D0603544

GREAT EXPLORATIONS

MARCO POLO

To China and Back

STEVEN OTFINOSKI

BENCHMARK BOOKS

MARSHALL CAVENDISH
NEW YORK

With special thanks to Professor Paul W. Mapp,
The College of William and Mary,
for his careful reading of this manuscript.

Benchmark Books
Marshall Cavendish
99 White Plains Road
Tarrytown, New York 10591-9001
www.marshallcavendish.com

Copyright © 2003 by Steven Otfinoski
Map copyright © 2003 by Marshall Cavendish Corporation
Map by Rodica Prato
All rights reserved.
No part of this book may be reproduced in any form without written permission of the publisher.

Library of Congress Cataloging-in-Publication Data
Otfinoski, Steven
Marco Polo : to China and back / by Steven Otfinoski
v.cm. – (Great explorations)
Contents: A distant world – A father's journey –Marco joins the adventure – Mountain and desert – The court of
Kublai Khan – A most trust aide – Escort for a princess – Strange homecoming – A prisoner of war – Marco mil-
lions.
ISBN 0-7614-1480-0
1. Polo, Marco, 1254-1323?—Journeys—China—Juvenile literature. 2. Explorers—Italy—Biography—Juvenile liter-
ature. 3. China—Description and travel—Juvenile literature. [1. Polo, Marco, 1254-1323? 2. Explorers. 3. Voyages
and travels. 4. Asia—Description and travel.] I. Title. II. Series.
G370.P9 O83 2002   915.04'2'092—dc21   2002000068

Photo Research by Candlepants Incorporated
Cover Photo: Art Archive
Cover Inset: Corbis/Bettmann

The photographs in this book are used by permission and through the courtesy of: *Art Archive*: 4, 19, 33, 34-35,
42, 49, 62, 67, 69. *Corbis*: Christie's Images, 7; Historical Picture Archive, 9; Bettmann, 10, 13, 16, 50, 55, 59, 65;
Hulton-Deutsch Collection, 27; Leonard de Selva, 57. *Art Resource*, NY: 17, 23,; Alinari, 8; Victoria & Albert
Museum, London, 15; Werner Forman Archive, 20-21, 24; Giraudon, 29, 39, 45, 61; Erich Lessing, 52; Scala, 56.

Printed in Hong Kong
1 3 5 6 4 2

Contents

The detail in this Italian map—drawn in 1449—shows the greatness of China in Kublai Khan's time.

foreword

When we think of explorers, we picture daring adventurers in search of new lands and peoples. We think of soldiers of fortune, bold navigators, and courageous men of action.

But one of the first western Europeans to reach China was none of these. Marco Polo was a merchant. He headed into the unknown with his father and uncle to trade goods and make money.

However, this young Venetian was brave, intelligent, and resourceful. He was also a keen observer of people and places. These qualities helped him survive the dangerous journey he made halfway around the world and made him the trusted aide to the most powerful king on earth.

Although he may not have seen himself as an explorer, Marco Polo was exactly that. His adventures and the book he wrote about them inspired generations of explorers and led indirectly to the discovery of the New World of the Americas.

This is his story.

ONE

A Distant World

Marco Polo was born in 1254 in the city-state of Venice. It was a very different time from our own. Europe was then a collection of tiny kingdoms ruled by warring lords and noblemen. The concept of a nation united under one ruler was still a new idea. Italy was not one country but a group of independent city-states. Venice was one of the most important of these city-states. Its wealth was built on trade with the East, or the Asian countries beyond the Mediterranean Sea. Venetian merchants and traders made their base of operations for trade with Asia in the city of Constantinople. This city was located at the western end of the Black Sea and was the gateway to the Middle East. Today it is called Istanbul and lies in present-day Turkey.

Middle Eastern merchants came to Constantinople and traded exotic spices, silks, jewels, and other goods from China and India. Well-

Venice, with its many canals, has always been a unique city. These small boats, called gondolas, are still used to transport people around the city.

to-do Europeans had enjoyed these goods for hundreds of years. However, few Europeans had journeyed to the lands they came from. The overland route to China, called the Silk Road, was filled with dangers. There were scorching deserts, ruthless bandits, and groups of people in constant warfare with one another. Besides this, the Catholic Church discouraged such travel. It considered the people of the East enemies of Christianity. For their part, the nations of central Asia did their best to prevent Europeans from crossing their lands. They wanted to keep their monopoly of the Eastern trade.

Among the most dreaded of these groups were the Mongols. These fierce warriors came out of present-day Mongolia, Manchuria,

VENICE, QUEEN OF THE SEAS

Venice is a city whose survival has always depended on the sea. Located on the Adriatic Ocean, the city was built on 118 islands connected by canals. During the fall of the Roman Empire, the islands were settled by refugees. The people of Venice lived by fishing and trade. They began trading with Constantinople and other Italian city-states in the ninth century. With its network of canals and Byzantine-styled buildings, Venice was one of the most exciting and lively cities in Europe by Marco Polo's time.

In the fifteenth century, Venice had become the most powerful of the Italian city-states, earning it the title the "queen of the seas." In 1453, Constantinople fell to the invading Turks, and the Eastern trading markets were closed. The discovery of America several decades later shifted the trading to the Atlantic Ocean and away from Venice and its enterprising merchants. Spain, Portugal, England, and France would become far more powerful trading nations by the sixteenth century.

Venice would be the queen of the seas no longer.

This seventeenth-century picture gives a bird's-eye view of Venice. Note the trading ships in the harbor.

Hagia Sophia, pictured here, was Constantinople's greatest cathedral. When the Turks conquered the city in 1453, it was turned into a Muslim mosque.

and Siberia in 1206. They quickly conquered China and much of Asia, led by their powerful warlord, Genghis Khan.

Over the next half-century, the Mongols built an empire that encompassed two-thirds of Europe and Asia. Years later, this is how Marco Polo described these mighty warriors in his book:

They are brave in battle, almost to desperation, setting little value upon their lives, and exposing themselves without hesitation to all manner of danger. Their disposition is cruel. They are capable of supporting every kind of privation [hardship], and when there is a necessity for it, can live for a month on the milk of their mares [female horses], and upon such wild animals as they chance to catch.

This engraving shows the fierceness and courage that made Genghis Khan a great warrior and conqueror.

But Genghis Khan was also a brilliant political leader and organizer of governments to run all his conquered lands. He placed each government under the rule of a khan, or king. All these khans owed their loyalty to him, the Great Khan.

While Europeans feared the Mongols, they were also fascinated by them. They were grateful that the Mongols had conquered the Muslims, their enemies in the Middle East. The Mongols also brought order and peace to Asia. They made the overland routes to China safe for travelers once more. The Europeans wondered if, in time, they might be able to convert the Mongols to Christianity and make them their allies.

Among the first to travel the overland route to the East at this time were two merchant brothers, Niccolo and Maffeo Polo—Marco's father and uncle. They left Venice around 1253, before Marco was born. They had traveled to Constantinople before, but this journey would take them much farther from home. The Polos planned to avoid the regular overland route. They decided to head north to trade with the nomads who lived above the Black Sea. As they set off on their journey, neither man could imagine just how far it would take them.

T W O

A father's Journey

Shortly after the Polos arrived in Constantinople, the city was caught in a wave of political upheaval. Venetians, Genoese, and Greeks were fighting each other to gain control of the city. The Polos sold all their trading goods—probably silks, spices and other Eastern products—and bought jewels. Jewelry, they decided, would be easy to transport if they had to leave suddenly. Then, with their jewels, they sailed across the Black Sea to the port city of Soldaia on the southern coast of present-day Ukraine.

The trading in Soldaia was not very good and they soon decided to leave. However, the route back home was dangerous due to a state of political anarchy and lawlessness. The Polos headed further eastward towards Southern Russia, hoping to avoid the fighting and find a way back to Venice. Quite by accident, they were approaching the outer reaches of the Mongol Empire and decided to sell their jewels to the khans.

Niccolo and Maffeo Polo setting out with a caravan during their
first journey to China

The two brothers were now in a region that was ruled by Barka
Khan, a grandson of the great Genghis Khan. The brothers met Barka
and gave him some of their jewels as a goodwill gift. The khan was
pleased and invited the Polos to stay in the city of Saurai for a year. They
also visited the city of Bulgar. Two years later, in the spring of 1262, Niccolo and Maffeo prepared to leave for home. Then Barka went to war
against his cousin Hulagu Khan of Persia, what is now present-day Iran,
probably over a territory dispute.

The Polos once more headed eastward to avoid danger. They rode
camels southeast into the desert and reached Bukhara, the trading cap-

ital of Persia. Today Bukhara is in present-day Uzbekistan. There the Polos spent their time learning the language and customs of the peoples around them.

While Niccolo and Maffeo were having these adventures, Marco's life in Venice was quite ordinary. After his mother died, young Marco went to live with his Aunt Flora. He grew up in her upper-class home in Venice's San Giovanni Christostimo district. He had a happy childhood, surrounded by aunts, uncles, and cousins.

Like the other children of his class, Marco Polo attended school only long enough to learn to read, write, and calculate. He was also trained to be a merchant and learned how to evaluate products and deal in foreign currency. Venice, with its docks and ships, was an exciting place for a boy to grow up. Marco loved listening to the colorful tales of the sailors and traders at the docks. He dreamed of sailing to distant shores himself.

Meanwhile, his father and uncle were becoming bored in the city of Bukhara, where they had remained for three years. One day an ambassador from Hulagu Khan's court arrived in Bukhara and was amazed to find two Westerners living there. The official was on his way to the court of the Great Kublai Khan. Kublai was another of Genghis Khan's grandsons. Genghis, who ruled from 1206 to his death in 1227, was succeeded by his son Ogotai, who died in 1241. There were several relatives of Ogotai who ruled briefly before Kublai Khan seized power in 1260.

The ambassador invited the Polos to accompany him to Kublai Khan's court. The Great Khan, he told them, was very interested in the West and would welcome the chance to talk to them.

The brothers accepted the invitation for two reasons—traveling with the ambassador's party would afford them safe passage out of Bukhara, and they figured they could sell most of their jewels at Kublai Khan's court.

Traveling by horse and ox-drawn cart, it took the Polos another year to reach the court of Kublai Khan in China, then called Cathay.

WARRIORS ON HORSEBACK

The Mongols' amazing success in conquering Asia was due in large part to their superb horsemanship. The Mongolian cavalry was an unstoppable war machine. Cavalrymen were able to fight fiercely while on horseback thanks to two inventions—stirrups and cruppers. The stirrups, first invented by the Chinese, held the rider's feet secure at the horse's side. Cruppers were leather straps that passed under the horse's tail to keep the saddle in place. Together, these pieces of equipment allowed the rider great freedom of movement.

Mongolian cavalrymen carried an arsenal of weapons. Light cavalrymen were equipped with a short bow and two quivers containing up to sixty arrows. They also were armed with a small sword, an axe, a dagger, and two javelins. Although the bow was short, it could hit an enemy target up to a distance of 350 yards (320 m).

Heavy cavalrymen were protected in battle by iron helmets and armor of layered leather. The armor covered them from their chin to their knees. They also carried shields of animal skin or wicker. Saddlebags made of hide were waterproof and could be inflated for crossing rivers.

Ready for anything, the Mongolian cavalry swept across Asia, conquering everyone in their path.

Mongol warriors were nearly invincible on their fast, sure-footed horses.

The Polo brothers appear before the great Kublai Khan.

The Great Khan welcomed the Westerners warmly at his summer palace at Shang-tu. He wanted to know all about life in Europe and was particularly curious about their religion, Christianity. The Polos were excited at this development. If Kublai Khan were to convert to Christianity it could lead to a strong alliance between the Mongols and the West. Christian missionaries had been sent to the Mongols in 1246 and 1253. They each reached the Mongols at their capital at Karakorum, delivered their teachings, and wrote what they saw. They noted that among the people they met in the city were other Europeans and Christians. The Polos were in the perfect position to aid this alliance.

Kublai Khan wrote a letter for the Polos to deliver to the Pope. In the letter, he requested that the Pope send one hundred Christian scholars to explain their religion to him. If he liked what he heard, Kublai Khan suggested he might convert himself and his people to Christianity. He also requested that the brothers return to his court with oil from the

Lamp of the Holy Sepulchre, which hung in the tomb of Jesus in Jerusalem. The oil was said to have magical powers.

Before they left, the khan gave the Polos golden tablets to carry with them. The tablets were a sign that they were under his protection wherever they traveled in his empire. In the spring of 1266, the two brothers began the long journey back to Venice. They would face storms, snow, mountains, and flooding along the way. The trip would take three long years.

In April 1269, they finally reached the port of Acre, now called Akko, in Israel. It lay north of Jerusalem on the eastern end of the Mediterranean Sea. Here they received news that Pope Clement IV had died only months before and a new pope had not yet been elected. Uncertain of what this would mean for their mission, the weary Polos continued on to Venice.

Kublai Khan gives the Polos gold tablets for protection on their journey home. The artist has inaccurately dressed the Khan and his attendants in European garb.

THREE

Marco Joins the Adventure

Marco Polo was fifteen when his father returned home. He was thrilled to have this father back, since he'd lost his mother at such an early age. He was entranced by stories of his father and uncle's adventures in the court of Kublai Khan. Now a young man, Marco yearned to have adventures of his own in distant lands.

Niccolo remarried and enjoyed his time with his son. But both he and Maffeo were impatient to return to the khan's court. They waited anxiously for news of the appointment of a new pope. Two years passed and the group of cardinals who elected the pope could not agree on a candidate. The Polos decided to wait no longer to return to China.

The brothers decided to take the willing seventeen-year-old Marco with them. They left Venice and journeyed back to Acre. Here they met with the church's legate, or representative, in the Holy Land, Teobaldo Visconti of Piacenza. Teobaldo was sympathetic to their predicament.

This highly stylized picture of Marco Polo's departure from Venice is taken from a book written about fourteen years after his death.

He wrote a letter to the Great Khan. He explained that their failure to return with the one hundred Christian scholars was not their fault. Only the Pope could make this decision, and there was as yet no new pope. He also gave the Polos permission to take the oil from the Lamp of the Holy Sepulchre that the khan had requested.

THE SILK ROAD

Traders had been traveling from Europe to China for a thousand years or more before the Polos headed east in 1271. The famous Silk Road was established in Roman times and linked the Roman Empire with ancient China. Chinese silk was highly prized by the Romans and they paid for it with gold. Yet, few of the traders who crossed the long, overland route were either Roman or Chinese. They were mostly Middle Eastern traders who served as the brokers between the two peoples.

Goods were not the only commodities that traveled along the Silk Road. Ideas and knowledge also traveled regularly

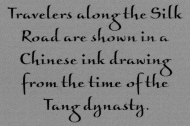

Travelers along the Silk Road are shown in a Chinese ink drawing from the time of the Tang dynasty.

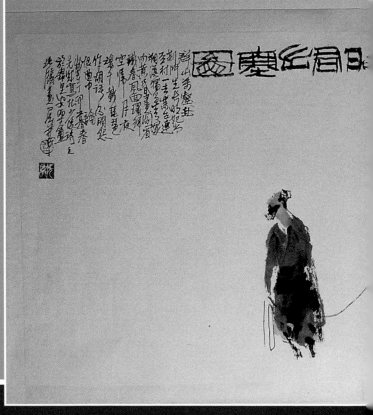

from East to West and back. The Silk Road was a first "information highway" and allowed ideas about religion, philosophy, and technology to travel.

The trading route flourished in China during the Han and Tang dynasties. After the Tang dynasty fell in A.D. 907, the road was closed for hundreds of years. The Mongols, conquerors of China, reopened it in the 1200s. But three centuries later Portuguese explorer Vasco de Gama completed a sea route to the East around Africa. Carrying goods by sea was far easier and safer than carrying them on land. By then the legendary Silk Road faded into history.

Armed with the oil and the letters, the Polos began the long journey back to China. Roadblocks delayed their progress. A messenger quickly caught up with them with amazing news. The cardinals had finally come to an agreement and had chosen a new pope. He was none other than Teobaldo himself!

The Polos rushed back to Acre where Teobaldo, now Pope Gregory X, greeted them warmly. He wrote new letters to the Khan as pope. He gave the Polos lavish gifts to present to Kublai Khan. Gregory also sent two Dominican friars to whom he gave papal power to accompany them. It was hardly the one hundred scholars the Khan had asked for, but at least they would not return empty-handed.

The Polos and the missionaries sailed to the coastal city of Ayas in present-day Armenia. Here they received distressing news. Egyptian Muslims had launched an invasion of the region. The Dominican friars were frightened and refused to go any farther. They handed over the papal letters to the Polos and returned to the safety of Acre under an escort of soldiers.

The Polos decided to continue despite the dangers. They headed north through the Caucausus Mountains, then turned south and crossed Persia. Along the way they saw some legendary sites. In Armenia they viewed Mt. Ararat. This was the place where Noah's Ark supposedly came to rest after the Great Flood in the Bible. They passed through Saba in Persia, the fabled home of the Three Wise Men who traveled to Bethlehem to honor the baby Jesus at his birth.

In Persia they joined a caravan for safety. They passed through mountains and entered the Rudbar Plain, a scorching desert. The caravan was attacked by the Karaunas, a group of ruthless bandits. Some of the party, including the Polos, escaped capture. The rest were killed or sold into slavery.

Marco Polo withstood every danger bravely with his father and uncle. He took detailed notes on everything he saw. He filled notebooks

The animal passengers leave Noah's Ark as it rests on Mt. Ararat after the Great Flood. Marco Polo passed by this legendary mountain on his way to China.

A Treasure House Called Asia

One of the driving forces that brought the Polos to the East was wealth. Compared to medieval Europe, the East was a treasure house of gold, silver, and precious stones.

Everywhere the three men traveled they were dazzled by mineral riches. In Malabar, India, divers extracted precious pearls from oysters in the Indian Ocean. In Khotan men unearthed jade from the dry riverbeds. Badakshan's mines brought forth a wealth of rubies, sapphires, and lapis lazuli.

Marco may have exaggerated slightly about the riches to be found in the East, but he was certainly awestruck by what he had seen. "The quantity of gold collected there exceeds all calculation and belief," he said of the island of Java.

Time and again, Marco noted meeting peoples who wore rings and bracelets of gold and silver. He saw gold in many forms—bullion, jewelry, and even woven into a kind of heavy cloth called brocade.

These reports of the fabulous wealth of Asia as recorded by Marco Polo inspired many nations and their explorers. It was one of the main reasons for the explosion of exploration that would follow several centuries later.

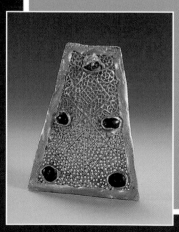

This fragment of gold-and-garnet jewelry is indicative of the wealth that dazzled the Polos and other Westerners who visited China.

with facts about the people in each region and their way of life. In one of his most interesting observations, he saw people collecting lamp oil from a hole in the ground in the Kingdom of Georgia.

Nine months after leaving Acre, the Polos reached the port of Hormuz on the Persian Gulf. From here they planned to sail across the Indian Ocean and head north to China. But when they saw the ships available to them they had second thoughts.

"Their ships are very bad," wrote Marco, "and many of them foundered [sank] because they were not fastened with iron nails but stitched together with thread made of coconut husks."

The Polos believed such fragile ships would fall apart in the first storm they encountered. They decided instead to travel overland to China, heading north across Asia. They would avoid the perils of the sea, but would find new dangers on land. They would also add months to their journey.

In September 1272—after surviving a hot summer in Hormuz—Marco Polo, his father, and his uncle finally headed north.

Marco, Niccolo, and Maffeo headed north through Persia to the Oxus River, now called the Amu Darya. They followed the river into Afghanistan, passing through green valleys and hot deserts. They reached the province of Badakhshan in the shadow of the large mountain range known as the Pamirs. At that time, the Pamirs were believed to be the world's tallest mountains. People called them the "Roof of the World."

Before the Polos could start their climb up the Pamirs, Marco grew ill. He may have gotten sick from bad water when crossing the desert. Whatever made him ill, he remained so for months. Niccolo and Maffeo wisely decided to stay in one place until Marco became better. They stopped at Badakshan in the foothills of the Pamirs. This province was famous for its ruby and sapphire mines. The brothers wanted to buy some rubies, but the lord of Badakshan forbade anyone from taking the rubies out of his country.

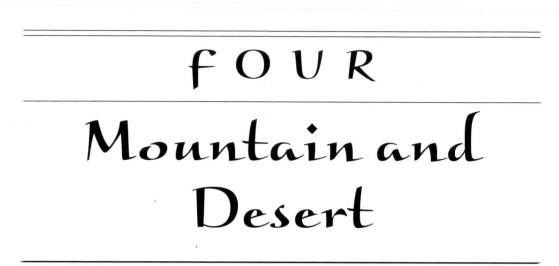

FOUR
Mountain and Desert

After nearly a year, Marco finally got better. His recovery was due at least in part to the air of the mountain plain, where his father and uncle had carried him. "The air is so pure," Marco later wrote, "that when those who dwell in the towns, and in the plains and valleys below, find themselves attacked with fevers . . . they immediately remove thither, and remaining for three or four days in that situation, recover their health."

Although Marco was now fit to travel, the journey was slow and treacherous. The Pamirs rise over 20,000 feet (6,097 m) above sea level. It took the Polos twelve days to cross them. There was little oxygen on the mountain plateau. The travelers found it difficult to start a fire. Cooking food also took much longer than at lower altitudes.

When they reached the bottom of the mountains, the party entered the thriving city of Kashgar. The region surrounding the city was fer-

Marco Polo's party may once have crossed this high mountain pass in Afghanistan.

tile. To the east, however, lay the last obstacle they would face before entering China—the Gobi Desert.

The Gobi is one of the world's largest deserts. It stretches across southern Mongolia and northern China covering more than 500,000 square miles (1,295,000 sq km). The Polos joined a caravan and bought camels and food supplies before setting out. The Gobi had a reputation for being haunted by ghosts, which Marco, for one, believed.

"If, during the daytime, any person remain behind on the road . . . they unexpectedly hear themselves called to by their names, and in a tone of voice to which they are accustomed," he wrote. "Supposing the call to proceed from their companions, they are led away by it from the

THE OLD MAN
OF THE MOUNTAIN

While traveling through the region of Tunokain before reaching the Pamirs, Marco Polo heard the legend of the ruler known as the "Old Man of the Mountain."

The "old man," Muslim leader Hasan-e-Sabbah, gained control of the mountain fortress of Alamut in 1090. To spread his power, he created a secret order of followers. Among his followers was a group called the devotees, who were trained to kill his enemies.

According to legend, Sabbah gave his devotees the drug hashish to bend them to his will. He promised them all the pleasures of paradise if they died while killing his enemies. Although Sabbah died in 1124, his army of killers spread terror across the mountains of Iran and Syria for more than a century.

Hulagu Khan finally captured the Old Man of the Mountain's fortress in 1256 as the Mongols extended their empire westward. Most of Sabbah's followers were wiped out by the

This highly fanciful picture shows the Old Man of the Mountain receiving his followers in a garden. It suggests none of the menace surrounding this legendary Muslim leader.

Mongols. A few of their descendents are said to survive to this day in northern Syria.

Marco Polo made the Old Man of the Mountain a notorious figure in Europe. Our English word "assassin" is derived from the word "hashish," the drug that Sabbah fed his killers. Today *assassin* refers to any person who murders a political or public figure.

PRESTER JOHN— ASIA'S LEGENDARY PRIEST KING

While he was anxious to reach the court of Kublai Khan, Marco was also eager to meet another fabled great Asian ruler. Prester John was said to be the Christian priest and king of a vast, rich empire in central Asia—and a member of a Christian Asian community called the Nestorian Church. It is doubtful that Prester John was anything more than a legend. The legend began in the twelfth century and may have sprung from the biblical figure John the Elder in the New Testament. Most Europeans during Marco Polo's time believed Prester John existed, and Marco refers to him a number of times in his book. He even speaks of certain provinces as "governed by princes of the race of Prester John."

Over the centuries, for some reason, Europeans relocated Prester John's kingdom from Asia to Africa. Ethiopia was often cited as his kingdom. His legend persisted at least through the fifteenth century. In the early part of the 1400s, Portugal's Prince Henry the Navigator even hoped to plan a crusade with Prester John if he ever made contact with him. Such a crusade, he believed, would once and for all drive the Muslims from the Holy Land. When Portuguese explorer Vasco De Gama reached Mozambique on the eastern coast of Africa in 1497, the local people told him he'd find Prester John's capital deep in the interior. De Gama never found the great white priest king. But the legend served a very practical purpose—it speeded the exploration of Africa, just as it had earlier done in Asia.

direct road and not knowing in what direction to advance, are left to perish."

The ghosts might have been imaginary, but the mirages of water some of the travelers saw appeared very real. They had to struggle to ignore these mirages or risk wandering off into the desert to die. The caravan moved slowly and averaged about nineteen miles (thirty km) a day. It took the Polos a month to cross the Gobi at its narrowest point.

Three and a half years after the Polos had left Venice, they were finally in sight of their goal. In the spring of 1275, soldiers met and escorted them to the Great Khan. It had been nine years since Niccolo and Maffeo Polo had last been in China. Forty days later they entered the city of Shang-tu, the summer home of Kublai Khan. It was located north of the present-day Chinese capital of Beijing. As they approached the great walls of the city, Marco Polo might well have thought about what wonders awaited them inside.

FIVE

In the Court of Kublai Khan

Kublai Khan was sixty years old when Marco Polo and his relatives arrived at his summer palace. Kublai Khan had been ruler of the Mongol Empire for fifteen years and was nearing the height of his power. Marco, now twenty-one years old, was much impressed with the Khan's person.

"[He] is neither tall nor short," he wrote. "His limbs are well formed, and in his whole figure there is a just proportion. His complexion is fair, and occasionally suffused [spread through] with red, like the bright tint of the rose. Which adds much grace to his countenance [face]. His eyes are black and handsome, his nose is well shaped and prominent."

The Great Khan was equally taken with Marco. He was especially fascinated by the young man's intelligence and energy. Marco knew four languages, was an excellent horseman, and was a captivating speaker. He told Kublai Khan vivid stories of the lands and peoples he

The "bright tint of the rose" Marco Polo described as marking Kublai Khan's complexion can be seen clearly in his portrait by an unknown artist.

had seen on their long journey. It was this last talent that would soon make Marco Polo an important member of the Mongolian court.

The Khan was highly pleased with the letters from the Pope and other gifts the Polos presented to him. He didn't seem upset that they had brought no Christian scholars. It is possible that Kublai Khan was more interested in Westerners as advisors and friends than as religious allies.

In another historically inaccurate European painting, Marco Polo stands before Kublai Khan, who resembles a European monarch.

The summer palace at Shang-tu was magnificent. Inside the marble palace wall was a private park surrounded by another wall that extended 16 miles (26 km). The park was filled with fountains, meadows, and brooks. It was also stocked with wild animals that the Khan hunted.

"Frequently, when he [Kublai Khan] rides about this enclosed forest, he has one or more small leopards carried on horseback, behind

BLACK STONES AND PAPER MONEY

Some historians have questioned whether Marco Polo ever traveled to China at all. They say this because his book fails to mention many important Chinese customs and places. These include the use of chopsticks, tea, the Chinese custom of binding females' feet from birth, Chinese writing, and the Great Wall of China.

Other historians have defended Marco. They say that he saw China largely through the eyes of its Mongol rulers. They claim he had little direct contact with the Chinese people.

There are, however, some specific aspects of Chinese life and technology that he did record. One of these is the strange "black stones" the Chinese burned like firewood. The stones burned far longer than wood and made an excellent fuel. The black stones were coal, something not widely used at the time in most of Europe.

One use for coal in China was to heat baths. The Chinese

their keepers," wrote Marco, "and when he pleases to give direction for their being slipped [let go], they instantly seize a stag or goat, or fallow [Eurasian] deer, which he gives to his hawks, and in this manner he amuses himself."

bathed daily in winter and three times a week in summer. Marco must have found this shocking. Venetians, like most Europeans, seldom bathed.

Another Chinese invention was paper money. Europe at that time only used coins as currency. They were heavy and impractical. Here Marco describes how paper money was made at the royal mint at Kanbalu:

He [Kublai Khan] causes the bark to be stripped from those mulberry-trees . . . and takes from it that thin inner rind which lies between the coarser bark and the wood of the tree. This being . . . pounded in a mortar, until reduced to a pulp, is made into paper . . . When ready for use, he has it cut into pieces of money of different sizes, nearly square, but somewhat longer than they are wide . . . The coinage of this paper money is authenticated with as much form and ceremony as if it were actually of pure gold or silver . . .

All in all, Marco Polo must have found the Chinese and their Mongol rulers to be far more civilized than the society he left behind in Europe.

At the end of the summer, the entire court moved south to the winter capital of Khan-balik, which means "city of the Great Khan." Today it is the city of Beijing. Back then, the city was divided into three concentric squares. The outer square was home to ordinary citizens and merchants. The second square was called the Tatar city. Here lived the khan's soldiers and bodyguards. The inner square was the imperial city. Here was the khan's palace and living quarters for members of his court.

The imperial palace at Khan-balik was even grander than the one at Shang-tu. Its walls were coated with gold and silver. Behind it was a man-made lake. Marco described it as "the greatest palace that ever was."

Great banquets for up to six thousand guests were held in the palace's dining hall. The servers wore silk handkerchiefs over their mouth and nose to prevent their breath from touching the food. The Great Khan, sitting above the other guests, drank kumiss, a beverage made from horses' milk, out of a golden goblet. After the meal was finished, jugglers and acrobats entertained the guests.

For all his wealth, Kublai Khan was sensitive to the needs of his people. When farmers had a bad year, he gave them food from his storehouses. When drought or disease killed their cattle, he replaced them from his own stock. The khan built hospitals and schools and was tolerant of the different religions practiced in his empire.

Despite this, Kublai Khan and the Mongols were not loved by their Chinese subjects. The Chinese did not enjoy the full rights of citizens and few of them were employed at court. The khan feared they would rebel and preferred to be surrounded by his fellow Mongols and foreigners. The Polos, among the few Westerners in China, were highly regarded by the khan. He gave them luxurious apartments and invited them to stay in his capital as aides and advisors.

The khan regularly sent envoys to the cities and provinces to report to him how the people lived and what they produced. Two years after Marco Polo arrived in China, the khan charged him with such a mission. It was an incredible honor for a young foreigner. The appointment

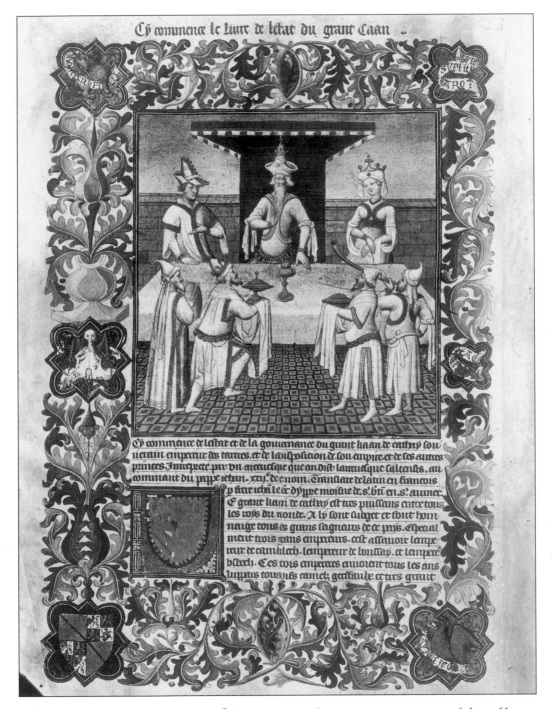

A medieval illustration of the Great Khan enjoying a meal hardly does justice to the grand banquets described in Marco Polo's book.

GETTING THE MAIL THROUGH

One of the most efficient features of the Mongol Empire was its postal system, which was inherited from the Chinese. It consisted of a network of post stations scattered throughout the empire's many provinces. Swift runners were sent on 3-mile (5-km) relays between stations. Important mail going longer distances was carried by riders on horseback. The system was similar to the Pony Express that existed in the United States from 1860 to 1861. Each postal station was from 25 to 30 miles (40 to 48 km) apart. The stationmaster would hear a bell jingle on the rider's saddle and know he was riding in. By the time the rider arrived, food and a fresh pony were waiting for him. Riders often ate and slept in the saddle to make better time. By these means, mail could travel as far as 373 miles (600 km) in just one day.

showed how much the khan thought of this able young man. In the years ahead, Marco Polo would travel throughout the vast Mongol Empire in the Great Khan's name.

SIX

A Most Trusted Aide

Kublai Khan's empire was vast. There was no way that he could visit every corner of it in person. Instead, he relied on officials to travel across his empire and to bring him back news of what was happening in each province.

Most of these officials brought back facts and statistics. This information was useful, but gave Kublai Khan little idea of what these places were really like. Marco Polo was different. He noticed and recorded interesting details. He told the khan colorful stories about the history and customs of each place and its people. He offered colorful descriptions of the wild animals and plants that lived there. Kublai Khan looked forward with great anticipation to Marco's return from each mission. Is it any wonder that he came to rely so much on this young Venetian?

On his first mission for the khan, Marco went to the remote province of Yunnan at the Tibetan border. He brought back news of a

This map, dated 1459, depicts Kublai Khan's kingdom, much of which Marco Polo traveled as the Great Khan's representative.

---

troubled government. However, the khan was probably just as interested, in Marco's description of "a huge serpent" he saw there.

> At the fore part, near the head, they have two short legs, having their claws like those of a tiger, with eyes larger than a four-penny loaf and very glaring. The jaws are wide enough to swallow a man, the teeth are large and sharp, and their whole appearance is so formidable, that neither man, nor any kind of animal, can approach them without terror . . . .

THE CITY OF HEAVEN

Of all the places he visited in the Mongol Empire, Marco Polo was most impressed by the city of Kin-sai in eastern China, known as the "City of Heaven." "The city is," he later wrote, "beyond dispute the finest and noblest in the world."

Kin-sai may have had as many as one and a half million people living in it. It was far larger than any European city Marco Polo knew. Yet like his native Venice, Kin-sai was made up of tiny islands connected by reportedly twelve thousand stone bridges. He went on to write:

Those [bridges] which are thrown over the principal canals and are connected with the main streets, have arches so high, and built with so much skill, that vessels with their masts can pass under them, whilst, at the same time, carts and horses are passing over their heads—so well is the slope from the street adapted to the height of the arch.

We now know that what Marco was describing was a crocodile.

Marco also noted many strange customs. In the province of Kangigu, for example, he witnessed the peculiar art of tattooing.

Both men and women have their bodies punctured all over, in figures of beasts and birds; and there are among them, practitioners whose

Marco Polo's Route

sole employment it is to trace out these ornaments with the point of a needle, upon the hands, the legs, and the breast. When a black coloring stuff has been rubbed over these punctures, it is impossible, either by water or otherwise, to efface [wipe out] the marks. The man or woman who exhibits the greatest profusion of these figures, is esteemed the most handsome.

One of the oddest customs he noted was in the province of Kardandan. Here child-rearing was shared by both parents in a way that would surprise Westerners even today.

As soon as a woman has been delivered of a child and rising from her bed, has washed and swathed the infant, her husband immediately takes the place she has left, has the child laid beside him, and nurses it for forty days. In the meantime, the friends and relatives of the family pay to him their visits of congratulation; whilst the woman attends to the business of the house, carries victuals [food] and drink to the husband in his bed, and suckles the infant at his side.

Marco Polo also toured Sichuan Province in southern China and northern Burma at the Khan's command. His father and uncle some-

---

Marco Polo dressed in a Tatar costume, complete with sword and bows and arrow.

Marco Polo's Route

times accompanied him on these fact-finding trips. Many other times he traveled by himself.

Today Kin-sai is called Hangzhou and is the capital of Zheijang province. In 1861, rebels destroyed most of its old buildings and the city was later rebuilt as a modern city. If Marco Polo were to return today to his "City of Heaven," he would not recognize it.

Marco became so trusted an aide that he claimed Kublai Khan appointed him governor of the Chinese city of Yangzhou for three years. Unfortunately, there is no historical record to support Marco's claim. It is possible that he was appointed an official in the city and exaggerated his position.

The years passed and the Polos grew in power and prestige at the khan's court. But in another way, they were also Kublai Khan's prisoners. Several times they had asked the khan for permission to return home to Venice, but the ruler gently refused to let them leave. He was too fond of their company, he said. By 1290, the Polos began to wonder if they would ever see their native Venice again.

SEVEN

Escort for a Princess

It was more than homesickness that made the Polos anxious to leave China. They were beginning to fear for their lives. Kublai Khan was now an old man in his seventies. Over the years, members of the Mongol court had grown to dislike the Polos. They were jealous of their influence with the Great Khan. If he were to die, these enemies might well take their revenge on the three foreigners. Besides that, the Khan's death would throw the empire into a state of chaos. Warring factions and possibly revolting Chinese would make travel impossible. Time was running out for the Polos to leave China.

In 1292 their chance finally came. Bulagen, the wife of Arghun, khan of Persia, was dying. In her will Bulagen requested that her husband marry another woman of her family line. Arghun planned to honor his wife's request but needed Kublai Khan's permission. He sent envoys to the khan, who also happened to be his great-uncle. The

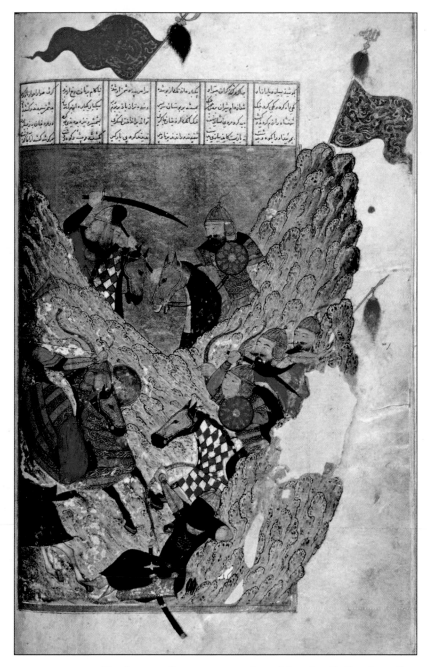

Constant fighting between tribes blocked the land route of the Persian envoy escorting Princess Kogatin and provided an opportunity for the Polos to return home to Venice.

A Legendary Bird

Not all of the fabulous animals Marco Polo wrote about in his book were real. For instance, he never saw a roc, but was told about it by the people of Madagascar, a large island off the eastern coast of Africa.

The roc is a huge legendary bird that appears in the tale of "Sinbad the Sailor" in the classic story collection *The Thousand and One Nights*.

"In form," Marco Polo wrote, "it is said to resemble the eagle, but it is incomparably greater in size; being so large and strong as to seize an elephant with its talons, and to lift it into the air, from whence it lets it fall to the ground, in order that when dead it may prey upon the carcass [dead body]."

Such secondhand accounts are sprinkled through Marco's book and are one of the reasons many people refused to believe his travels were real. Today, historians have been able to separate fact from fiction in this fascinating work.

The legendary roc, describes by Marco Polo, is seen here carrying Sinbad the sailor in an illustration from the classic story collection The Thousand and One Nights.

envoys asked Kublai Khan to choose a suitable wife for Arghun. The Great Khan was flattered and picked out a beautiful seventeen-year-old princess named Kogatin. The envoys and Kogatin began the return trip to Persia, but warring tribes blocked the way. The Persian party came back. They debated whether to wait or attempt the journey home by sea.

By coincidence, Marco Polo had just returned from a mission to India. Arghun's envoys were greatly impressed by Marco's knowledge of the sea routes through the Ocean. They pleaded with Kublai Khan to allow Marco, his father, and his uncle to help guide them back to Persia by sea. The khan was reluctant to let the Polos go, but he was also reluctant to offend his great-nephew. He finally allowed them to go with one condition—that they return to China once they had safely taken the princess to Persia.

The khan gave the Polos two golden tablets with his seal to guarantee their safe passage through his empire. Regardless of what the khan commanded, the Venetians had no intention of returning. But they wanted to take the wealth they had earned in the khan's service with them. They converted their possessions to jewels and sewed the stones into the linings of their clothes. This would hide them from bandits and pirates.

In 1292, after seventeen years in the Mongol Empire, the Polos set sail from the port city of Zaitun—now Xiamen—in southern China. Their fleet consisted of fourteen ships carrying six hundred people and enough provisions for two years. They sailed across the South China Sea to Ziamba, present-day Vietnam. Then they proceeded to the island of Java, part of what is today Indonesia. They arrived just as the monsoon season was beginning. The heavy rains and winds of the monsoon made sea travel unsafe. The party was forced to take cover on the large island of Sumatra. In the five months they spent on Sumatra, they saw many strange plants and animals.

Marco reported nuts "the size of a man's head, containing an edible substance that is sweet and pleasant to taste, and white as milk." Inside the nut was "a liquor as clear as water, cool, and better flavored and more delicate than wine or any other kind of drink whatever." Today we call this a coconut.

Marco Polo was one of the first Westerners to see and describe a rhinoceros. This detailed etching is by the German artist Albrecht Dürer.

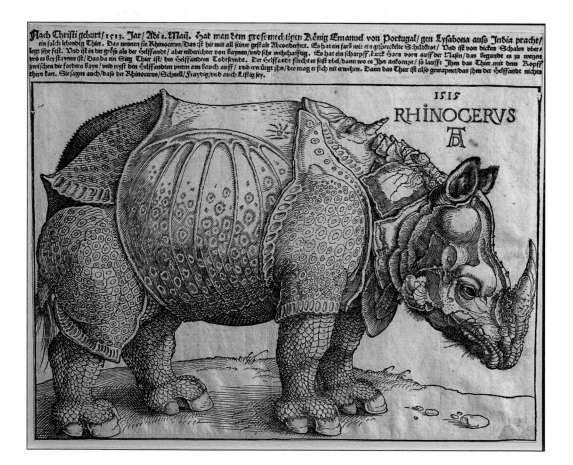

Marco also discovered a strange beast he mistook for the legendary unicorn. "Their hide resembles that of a buffalo," he wrote. "In the middle of the forehead they have a single horn . . . Their head is like that of a wild boar and they carry it low to the ground. They take delight in muddy pools, and are filthy in their habits."

Of course what Marco Polo described is a rhinoceros.

The monsoon season finally ended, and the fleet sailed on into the Indian Ocean and southwest to Ceylon, now Sri Lanka. Then they followed the Indian coast all the way to the Persian Gulf.

The trip was difficult and dangerous. By the time the fleet sailed into the Persian Gulf and the Straits of Hormuz, only eighteen of the six hundred people who had left China were still alive, according to Marco Polo's account. The survivors included the three Polos, Marco's Mongol slave, Pietro, and the princess. The others had all perished from disease, storms, and pirate attacks.

When they arrived in Persia they learned shocking news. Arghun Khan, whom Princess Kogatin had traveled so far to marry, was dead. His brother Kaikhatu now sat on the Persian throne. Kaikhatu suggested that the princess stay and marry his nephew, Arghun's son Ghazan. This seemed like a good idea and the party traveled to northern Persia where Ghazan was stationed. He readily agreed to take Kogatin as his bride. The couple later would rule as king and queen of Persia.

Their duty done, the Polos prepared to continue on to Venice despite their promise to the khan. Their parting with Kogatin was a sad one. They had shared many adventures and hardships with her. She regarded the three men as her protectors. Marco remembered her as "a very beautiful and charming person."

EIGHT

Strange & Homecoming

The Polos still had hundreds of miles to travel before they reached Venice. The dangers of the journey were far from over. From Hormuz they proceeded by camel across Persia to Trebizond, a Greek colony on the southern shores of the Black Sea. In the years since they had left Venice the rivalry between Venice and Genoa, another Italian city-state, had grown tense.

The Polos quickly sailed across the Black Sea to Constantinople, where the Greeks were also now in control. From there they traveled to Negroponte in Greece and finally arrived in Venice sometime in 1295.

They had been gone for twenty-four years, nearly a quarter century, and had traveled 15,000 miles (24,100 km). Venice was a different city than when they had left it. The Polos were different men. Years of travel and exposure to the sun had darkened their skin. They looked more like Asians than Venetians. Their clothes were worn and ragged.

A middle-aged Marco Polo as he might have looked on his return to Venice

They had not used Italian in years and spoke it haltingly, like foreigners.

Legend has it that when they reached their home, the Polos' own relatives didn't recognize them. They refused to believe they were who they said they were. The three men supposedly invited their families to a great banquet. They appeared at the banquet cleaned and dressed in radiant robes, at which time their relatives recognized them. When the meal ended, they disappeared and returned in their ragged clothes. As the stunned guests watched, they ripped open the lining of their clothing and out poured a fortune in precious stones of every size and color.

Family and friends now accepted the Polos for who they were, but they were not ready to believe their adventures. Most Venetians had never been out of the Mediterranean region. It was their entire world. Marco's tales of the fabulous palaces and cities of Kublai Khan's empire

GENOA: VENICE'S GREAT RIVAL

Genoa, like Venice, drew its power from the sea and trading. Founded by the Romans in about 200 B.C., it was the headquarters for the Roman fleet. When the Roman Empire fell, Genoa evolved into an independent city-state. By the tenth century, it developed a strong navy to defend itself from Muslim invaders from Spain and Egypt.

By the 1200s, Genoa largely controlled the central Mediterranean Sea. It began a series of wars with Venice for control of the eastern Mediterranean. Although Genoa had the upper hand for a time, it eventually lost the war to Venice in 1380. It also lost much of its power in the Peace of Turin signed the following year. The rise of the Turks in the east and internal conflicts reduced Genoa's power even further.

Today Genoa is Italy's largest port and a major industrial center.

This sixteenth-century view of Genoa shows the naval power that helped make it Venice's rival on the seas.

A noble Venetian from Marco Polo's time

NOBLE VÉNITIEN
XII⁰ SIÈCLE

were incredible to them. But even though people flocked to Marco's house to hear of his adventures, many thought they were largely made up.

The world of Venice was as strange to Marco as the world he described was to his listeners. Now forty-two years of age, he found life in Venice boring and meaningless. Unlike his father and uncle, he was not ready to settle down into a comfortable retirement. Unlike Niccolo, he had no wife or children to return to. For years he had been an important member of Kublai Khan's court. Now Marco Polo was just another Venetian merchant. It was not an easy adjustment.

Just as Marco was establishing himself as a merchant, war broke out between Genoa and Venice. All trade between the two cities and the outside world abruptly ended. At odds as to what to do with himself, Marco Polo began the last great adventure of his life.

NINE

A Prisoner of War

Sometime after war broke out, Marco Polo offered his services to the Venetian navy. The navy was impressed with his years of experience at sea, so they appointed him the gentleman commander of a war galley ship. As such, Marco would not actually command the ship of about 250 men, but would be a consultant to the ship's masters.

The mission of these privately owned ships was to protect Venetian harbors. Soon, Marco's ship became engaged in a sea battle with the Genoese. Historians differ as to exactly when and where this battle took place. Some believe it was the Battle of Curzola in the Adriatic Sea, one of the biggest naval battles to take place in the Middle Ages.

On September 7, 1298, about two hundred galleys and big ships participated in the sea battle. The Genoese emerged the victors. Eighteen Venetian galleys were sunk and sixty-six were captured. Reportedly, Marco Polo fought bravely. According to one account, "He was cap-

Marco Polo's galley is shown going up against the Genoese at the historic battle of Curzola in 1298.

tured because he threw himself and his galley to the front of the battle and because he was fighting for his country with great courage, and then injured, in chains, he was taken off to Genoa."

Polo was one of more than seven thousand Venetians taken prisoner. He was kept in an underground room in Genoa's Palazzo de San Giorgio. Other gentlemen of rank and wealth were released for ransom. But for some reason, his father and uncle's efforts to win Marco's release failed. Looking back, this may have been fortunate. It led Marco to help write the book that would make him famous.

Prison life for Marco Polo was not particularly hard, but it was boring. With so much time on their hands, the prisoners began telling each

BOOKS MADE BY HAND

Soon after his return to Venice from Genoa, Marco Polo became a published author. "Published" is perhaps not the most accurate word. The printing press and movable type would not be invented for another 150 years. *A Description of the World* had to be copied laboriously by hand.

Handwritten books had a long tradition in medieval Europe. Professional writers called scribes wrote or copied most books on sheets made from animal skin called parchment. They decorated the pages with elaborate, colorful designs and pictures. These early books were works of art as well as literature.

Rustichello, who had previously written two romances about King Arthur, wrote the book in Old French. This was the language used for literary works in Italy at that time. But Rustichello did not simply record Marco's adventures, he embroidered the tales with his own romantic writing style.

other stories to entertain themselves. Marco had been a spellbinding storyteller since his days at the court of Kublai Khan. His stories of life in the Mongol Empire soon made him a prison celebrity. The prisoners would gather daily to hear him tell of his adventures. Word spread of his storytelling outside the prison, and eventually the Genoese were coming to the Palazzo de San Giorgio just to hear him.

By Marco Polo's time, parchment was being replaced by paper made of cotton and linen. The demand for books increased as more people could afford them. Books were copied less decoratively so more copies could be made more quickly.

When movable type and the printing press were developed in the mid-1400s, printers tried to recreate the look of the handmade books. They used large type to resemble handwritten letters. Many pages of these printed books were still decorated by hand.

Among the first books to be printed on the new presses were the Bible and Marco Polo's book. Now more literate people could read about Marco Polo's adventures, when previously they had been enjoyed by only a privileged few.

This page from an early edition of Marco Polo's books shows the incredible decorative detail that went into hand-made books before the printing press's invention.

Among the other prisoners was a man from Pisa—a writer named Rustichello. A prisoner of the Genoese for ten years, Rustichello was as entranced as everyone else by Marco Polo's stories. He told Marco that if he would dictate his stories to him, he would write them down. The idea delighted the Venetian, and he sent a message to his father asking him to send the notebooks he wrote in

This is the illustrated title page from the first printed
edition of The Travels of Marco Polo, published in
Germany in 1477.

China to the prison. Soon Marco Polo and Rustichello were collaborating on a book.

Rustichello boastfully called the book *A Description of the World*. In time, it became better known as *The Travels of Marco Polo*.

The book was divided into three sections. The first part was a brief synopsis of Marco's travels to and from China. It included descriptions of places he passed through on his way to Kublai Khan's court. In the second part, Marco praised the virtues and leadership abilities of the Great Khan. He also described the people and lands ruled by him. The last part is devoted to Marco's return trip, especially the peoples of India.

From the first page of the prologue, Rustichello makes a strong case for Marco's groundbreaking travels. He calls Marco "a wise and learned citizen of Venice." He then claims that "from the creation of Adam to the present day, no man, whether pagan, or Saracen, or Christian . . . ever saw or inquired into so many and such great things as Marco Polo . . ."

The two men completed their work in the spring of 1299. About the same time a truce ended the war between Venice and Genoa. Marco Polo was released from prison after at least one year and said good-bye to Rustichello. He returned to Venice with the manuscript that would soon make him famous throughout Europe.

T E N

Marco Millions

Copies of *A Description of the World* circulated rapidly. All of Venice was talking about this fabulous work.

No traveler had gone so far from home before and come back to tell about such wonders. Indeed, one later editor retitled the work, *The Book of Marvels*. Another called it *Il Milione*, meaning "The Million." Marco's tendency to talk about the greatness and wealth of Kublai Khan in millions instead of thousands led people to shake their heads in disbelief. They wondered if everything in Marco's book was made up. People around Venice began calling him "Marco of the Million" or "Marco Millions." His home became known as "Millions Court."

Despite his newfound celebrity, Marco returned to life as a merchant. At the age of forty-five, he married a young noblewoman, Donata Badoer. They had three daughters. While he earned his living as a merchant, he probably found more satisfaction in his role as author and storyteller.

Marco Polo—fearless and unrepentant in old age.

MARCO POLO'S HEIR: CHRISTOPHER COLUMBUS

Among the most avid readers of Marco Polo's book in the fifteenth century was Genoese sea captain and navigator Christopher Columbus. Columbus was greatly impressed by Marco's description of the riches of Japan, one of the places Marco had never personally visited.

While Marco Polo sailed eastward to return to Europe from China, Columbus believed he could reach Japan by sailing westward across the Atlantic Ocean. Of course, neither man realized two continents blocked the way to the East. This is how Columbus came to discover the Americas.

Among the few books Columbus took along on his famous voyage in 1492 was a Latin translation of *The Travels of Marco Polo*. It survives today with Columbus' own notes in the margins. As further proof that Columbus took Marco Polo seriously, he carried letters with him from the king and queen of Spain. They were addressed to "The Great Khan of Cathay." Neither they nor the explorer probably realized that the last Mongol had been driven from China more than one hundred years earlier.

The young Christopher Columbus, inspired by the
writings of Marco Polo, dreams of reaching the East
by a new sea route.

In 1300, Niccolo Polo died. Ten years later, Marco's uncle Maffeo also passed away. Now Marco Polo was the only survivor of that extraordinary adventure. He felt increasingly alone and isolated.

The continuing success of his book comforted him, however. The book was translated into the Italian dialect of Tuscan. The Dominican priest and chronicler Francesco Pipeno of Bologna translated it into Latin. In 1307, the brother of French king Philip IV personally asked Marco for a copy of his book.

That same year Pope Clement V banned all trading with Muslims in Asia because they were enemies of Christianity. This did not stop the merchants of Italy from trading with the East. A much more dramatic event in the Mongol Empire, however, did just that.

Kublai Khan had died of old age in 1294, not long after the Polos left China. His descendants, who ruled the empire for three decades after him, were weak and degenerate. By 1328 the empire would be divided by civil war. The Chinese, under the Ming Dynasty, would rebel. The Mongol Empire was crumbling. Law and order broke down. Travel throughout the Middle East was becoming as dangerous as it had been before the Mongols came to power.

With the Middle East in turmoil, no one could follow Marco Polo's path to China now. No one could prove or disprove the wonders he claimed to have seen. So Marco Polo grew to old age a notorious figure, admired by some and scorned by others. Ill and dying, he prepared his last will. He freed his Mongol slave Pietro. He gave his golden tablets, the ones given to him by the Great Khan, to his daughters.

According to one story, a priest encouraged Marco Polo to take back his stories on his deathbed to save his soul. Marco supposedly looked at the priest and lifted himself up in the bed. "I did not tell half of what I saw," he said, "for I knew I would not be believed." Unrepentant to the end, Marco Polo died on January 8, 1324 in his bed at age seventy. He was buried alongside his father in the cemetery of the church of San Lorenzo.

The conquest of Constantinople by the Turks forever changed the medieval world that Marco Polo knew.

"Marco Millions" was dead. But his book lived on. By the 1500s, Marco Polo's book had been translated into nearly every language in Europe, including German, Spanish, English, Portuguese, and Gaelic.

Every well-read gentleman and scholar had his own copy. With time, more and more people came to believe that Marco Polo had told the truth.

Among the strongest believers was a new generation of European explorers. They yearned to reach the fabulous treasures of the East that Marco Polo had written about so vividly. Among these bold men were the Portuguese sea captain Vasco de Gama and a Genoese navigator named Christopher Columbus.

Marco Polo opened a new world of wonders to the people of Europe. He showed that the inhabitants of the East were not ignorant savages, but civilized people. He helped spread the use in Europe of coal, paper money, and such Eastern foods as rice and noodles.

More importantly, he created a new interest in the outside world that eventually led in the sixteenth century to the golden age of discovery. His bold spirit, love of adventure, keen intelligence, and eye for detail made him the first great explorer of the modern era.

Marco Polo and His Times

1253-1269 Niccolo and Maffeo Polo travel to China and back for the first time

1254 Marco Polo born in Venice

1271 Marco leaves Venice for China with his father and uncle

1275 Arrives at the summer palace of Kublai Khan, ruler of the Mongol Empire

1276-1292 Serves Kublai Khan, visiting far-flung parts of the Mongol Empire

1292 Leaves China with elder Polos to escort a princess to Persia

1294 Kublai Khan dies

1295 Arrives back in Venice, having been gone for 24 years

1298-99 Captured in sea battle by enemy Genoese and held a prisoner

1298-99 Writes *A Description of the World* with Pisan author Rustichello

1300 Father Niccolo Polo dies

1307 Pope Clement V bans all trade with Muslims in Asia

1324 Marco Polo dies at age 70

1328 Civil war breaks out in the Mongol Empire

1492 Christopher Columbus discovers America while searching for Japan, inspired by *The Travels of Marco Polo*

FURTHER RESEARCH

Books

Bandon, Alex. *The Travels of Marco Polo.* Austin, TX: Raintree Steck-Vaughn Publishers, January 2000.

Herbert, Janis. *Marco Polo for Kids.* Chicago: Chicago Review Press, August 2001.

MacDonald, Fiona. *Marco Polo: A Journey Through China.* Danbury, CT: Franklin Watts, Inc., August 1998.

Websites

Marco Polo

www.geography.about.com/cs/marcopolo/index.htm?iam=dpile&terms=MarcoPolo

www.carmensandiego.com/products/time/marcoc06/marcopolo.html

Kublai Khan

http://www.who2.com/kublaikhan.html

The Battle of Corzula (Korcula)

http://www.korcula.net/mpolo/mpolo700.htm

BIBLIOGRAPHY

Greene, Carol. *Marco Polo: Voyage to the Orient.* Chicago, IL: Children's Press, 1987.

Hull, Mary. *The Travels of Marco Polo.* San Diego, CA: Lucent Books, 1995.

Kent, Zachary. *Marco Polo.* Chicago: Children's Press, 1992.

Polo, Marco. *The Travels of Marco Polo.* New York: Orion Press, 1958.

Rosen, Mike. *The Travels of Marco Polo.* New York: Bookwright Press, 1988.

Stefoff, Rebecca. *Marco Polo and the Medieval Explorers.* New York: Chelsea House, 1992.

Source Notes

Chapter 1

p. 9 "They are brave in battle . . ." Marco Polo, *The Travels of Marco Polo*, p. 87.

Chapter 3

p. 24 (new) "The quantity of gold collected . . ." Marco Polo, *The Travels of Marco Polo*, p. 272. (Garden City Publishing Co. edition, 1930.)

p. 25 "Their ships are very bad . . ." quoted in Mary Hull, *The Travels of Marco Polo*, p. 43.

Chapter 4

p. 26 "The air is so pure . . ." Polo, p. 57.

p. 27 "If, during the daytime, any person . . ." Polo, p. 68.

p. 30 "governed by princes of the race . . ." Polo, p. 21 (Garden City).

Chapter 5

p. 32 "[He] is neither tall nor short . . ." Polo, p. 119.

p. 35 "Frequently, when he [Kublai Khan] rides about . . ." Polo, p. .

p.37 "He [Kublai Khan] causes the bark to be stripped . . ." Polo, pp. 153-154.

p. 38 "the greatest palace that ever was." Quoted in Zachery Kent, *The World's Great Explorers: Marco Polo*, p. 61.

Chapter 6

p. 42 "At the fore part, near the head . . ." Polo, p. 191.

p. 43 "Both men and women . . ." Polo, p. 205.

p. 43 "The city is beyond dispute . . ." quoted in Kent, p. 86.

p. 43 "Those [bridges] which are thrown over . . ." Polo, pp. 229-230.

p. 44 "As soon as a woman . . ." Polo, p. 194.

Chapter 7

p. 50 "in form, it is said to resemble the eagle . . ." Polo, p. 313.

p. 52 "the size of a man's head . . ." Polo, p. 275.

p. 53 "Their hide resembles that of a buffalo . . ." Polo, p. 274.

p. 53 "a very beautiful and charming person." quoted in Kent, p. 93.

Chapter 9

p. 58 "He was captured because he threw himself . . ." Website: 700th Anniversary of Battle of Korcula, http://www.korcula.net/mpolo/mpolo700.htm

p. 63 "a wise and leading citizen of Venice . . ." Polo, Prologue.

Chapter 10

p. 68 "I did not tell half . . ." Kent, p. 119.

INDEX

Page numbers in **boldface** are illustrations.